Hymns of a Mountain Girl

Hymns of a Mountain Girl

Huma Adnan

HYMNS OF A MOUNTAN GIRL
Copyright 2016 © Huma Adnan

No part of this publication may be reproduced, distributed, or transmitted in any form or by any means, including photocopying, recording, or other electronic or mechanical methods, without the prior written permission of the author except in brief quotations embodied in critical reviews, citations, and literary journals for non-commercial uses permitted by copyright law. For permission request email the author. humaadnan87@hotmail.com with the body:
"Attention: Permissions Coordinator"

Editor:
christinastrigaseditingservice@gmail.com
www.christinastrigas.com

Cover Art by:
Mitch Green

ISBN: 978-0-9979824-0-4

To
Adnan,
A man who knows how to bear and love a poet.

Table of Contents

Section One:

Love in Darkness	13
Roaring Father	14
Toyshop	16
Rain in a Desert	19
Fornicator	20
Termites	22
Beast	24
Chase in the Jungle	27
Destruction	28
Loss	29
Death of Silence	30
Final Goodbye	33
Wreckage	34
A Note to Suicide	35
Lost Love	36

Ego	38
Eulogy	40
Perfection	42
Demons	44
Adieu!	45
Seeking Cure	46
My Apple Tree	47
Irony	48
Infatuation	49
If You	50
Drowned	52
Haunting Memories	53
Wild Goose Chase	56
Deception	56
Achievement	58
Unsung	61
Love and Hunger	62

I No More Cage Goodness	65
The Girl Inside	67
Horse Race	70
The Lost Past	72
Compose New Song	74
Pain	75
You're Still Here	78
Tombstone	79
Library	81
Barriers of Sects	83
I Cut the Roots of Love	85
Reversal	86
Section Two	
Pronoun	87
Change	89
Two Words	92
Promise	94

Knock	95
Worries	96
Letter	98
Sea	100
Life's Art	101
Games	104
Child	105
Reader's Soul	107
Free Bird	109
Treader	111
Peace	113
Sonnets for Me	114
Erudite	116
Only Me	119
Heaven	120
Probably	121
Karma	125

Burning Hearts	127
Question	128
Three Tricky Words	131
Just Love	132
Come	133
Ashes	134
Letter to My Girl	135
You have	137
Don't Rot Your Soul	138
Love over Lust	139
Immortal	140
Survivor	141
Differences and Our Love	143
Light Your World	144
Butterfly	146
Words of Love	148
I Love You Mercilessly	149

Magician!	151
You are Sunshine!	153
Reunion	156
Jinx	159
Trust Your Instincts	161
Enemies	162
One Day	164
On the Peak	165
His Voice	167
My Poetry	168
Still Loved	169
Reader	170
Healer	171
Prayer	173
A Tribute to a Fierce Lover	174
Pleasure	176
Take Me Away	177

Normal Life	179
Moth	180
Daddy's Boy	181
Lover of Glow	184
Promise	186
Love Him	187
Unloved	188
After Years	189
Unaware	191
Glitter and Light	192

Section Three

Love and Something	193
Love Flows	194
Expiry date	195
Cherish Each Moment	196
Listen	198
Unfathomable Relation	200

Memories	201
The Way We Love	202
Right Love	203
Love Will Do	204
Bond	205
Wait	206
The Artist	207
Loving One's Self	208
Embracing Morning	210
Hope and Love	211
Bomb Blast	212
Kodak	215
My Land	217
War	219
Park	221
My Soul	222

Section One
Love in Darkness

Roaring Father

What is it to grow up in a house
where there lives a roaring father?
You start finding solace
in each lullaby sang to you
by everyone.
You start loving the tales
filled with fantasy.
You don't want to come back
to reality
because you have seen enough.
You don't let people tell you
how fake love can be.

You just want to believe
that each soothing lullaby
is actually meant for you.
You need a deep sleep
after all those roaring sounds.

Toyshop

A pain of looking through the window pane
of a toy shop is something
terrible a child feels.
I felt that pain arouse in my heart
several times while holding
Daddy's finger and peeping
inside the toy shop.
The colourful world
mesmerized me.
I never dared
to look at the price tag.
I never found
the courage to ask Daddy.
The candy doll would shout at me

'Come and hold me.'
The cheerful kids
going out of the shop
with Mickey Mouse bags,
their giggles yelled at me,
'Oh you see! How lucky we are!'
That pain would rise
like a strong tide,
filled my eyes
with salty burning water
and heat up my ears like lava
boiling in dead volcanoes.
It was the only terrible pain until
The day I saw
Daddy buying her kids
the biggest teddy bear,
Superman puzzle

and Nintendo.
I was stunned,
jealous
and that was when
I became an introvert
for the rest of my life.
Today, with all the money
in my account
I can buy as many teddies as I like
but can I buy a Daddy?

Rain in a Desert

Far away on some land
where people complain
when it rains and snows,
I walk by the lane and
let the sun scorch my skin.
I wonder does it rain
once a year
because
clouds are formed
with our
evaporated skin,
or do tears shed
during dark lonely
melancholic nights?

Fornicator

All afternoon she lets her body
be caressed by those hands
which are not hers.
She kept shutting out
the thoughts of guilt
tried not to focus on
spirits chanting,
fornicator, fornicator.
In the evening,
when she came back home
covered in cloth
from head to toe,
she tried to avoid
indubious eyes

and exclaimed before she was asked,
I'm not going to have a dinner,
I had the big meal with my friend after class.

Termites

You think she loves you?
No dear,
she loves the garlic bread
served at Pizza Hut.
She loves the movie shows
and lets you play with her
during movies
because you pay for tickets
and nachos.
At least you deserve
that little entertainment,
don't you?
Do you still think she
loves you?
She loves a new Gucci bag

and her increasing collection
of Mac
paid on your bank card.
When her friends visit
she shows them all
the brands and says,
'See what my uncle got me.'
And you think she loves you
while termites feed
on your bed.

Beast

That particular day when he left,
to heal my wounds
I resided
in the arms of a beast
who was in saint's cloak.
Too weak to fight for myself,
too broken to bring Love back,
I let the beast take me,
to make me forget him.
I let my body be a dessert
for the starving beast
who ate me bit by bit
licking his fingers
his desire grew and
he forgot he took me in his arms

to shelter me.
But to feed his devil,
he put his hairy hand
on my mouth.
Forgetting that I cried,
for one who left.
Yet
the pain of one gone
was far greater than
the pain the beast brought.
Once the beast was no longer hungry,
he drank two cans of beers,
burped and fell asleep.

I ran and reached back to his home
peeped inside the window and saw
him making love to her.

I felt better.
I forgot the beast.
This pain was better
than the beast's desire.

I triumph over trusting,
wrong shadows twice.

Chase in the Jungle

I wonder what deer
chase in the jungle?
Do they fall in love
with carnivores?
Are they too eaten up
by the ones they love
or left to be decayed
unsung?

Destruction

He chose to call me half a soul but I have realized I'm just composed of flesh and blood and he is my entire soul. Either he constructs or destructs me there's nothing which can take him away from my heart.

Loss

She is being questioned,

who stole the spark from her eyes
the soul from her smile?

She is fighting back her tears holding her heart tightly
she just asks,

Does that really matter when that loss was greater than the sparks and smiles?

Death of Silence

Silence dies inside me.
The world will not cry with me.
Terror or tears,
are not simple.
Cry deep in an ocean
or in a temple.
Things will not change,
neither can I anymore.
The world will not wait
nor do I have any haste for.

Sublime the darkness
into a river of fate.
Glow glorious in
death and fame.

Tremble or try to put
wind into your soul.
It will not come back
into glories
all which has
gone long before.

Shush!!!

Things which never have been
mine
silence cannot bring them.
Screaming and shattering
is an invalid option.
Fly into a darkness of clouds
jump into a green sea,
this will not change
the color of the moon,

whose identity bleeds,
not in red water,
but with wine filled with salt.

Oh man!
Requisition is fake.
Resolution is never made.
Restriction is thy fate.

Trust or hide the lie!
Neither be pure nor corrupt.
To be a sinner or preacher
was undecided.
To be a lover or enemy
is undecided.
To be human or beast
will be undecided.
Silence died inside me..

Final Goodbye

And I bid you a final good bye.
In the cosmos I shall meet you again,
in a hundred faces,
with a hundred souls,
and I would fall in love with you
a hundred times,
to reach the ladder of Divine.

Wreckage

All our lives we believe
we need to fall in love
to save our souls
to save our future.
Love can't save.
the one who loves or
one who is loved.
Love is just a pillar.
letting us stand firm
in sunshine or dark nights.
But if the earth shakes
love won't save us
from breaking down.
It would cry silently
on our wreckage.

A Note to Suicide

And if you would have trusted me,
leaving the world wouldn't be the
decision you would have made.
Once only,
you could have asked me,
the depth of my heart,
the Love I withhold.
Birds didn't mourn,
people didn't show up,
but a soul
who loved you
sits in the cemetery
carves your name on each stone.

Lost Love

Do you remember those chronic days,
when I'd sit out on the porch and wait?
The mourning moon was my only company,
solitude was made for me, mandatory.
If it were your words only,
I would have mended them long ago.
You made me share my residence,
the love and heart of yours.
Now she's gone
you knock the door,

since when did you start kneeling
in the cold?

'Move on my dear!' That's what
you said.
Here I forgive you and repeat your
words.
Remorse and contrition might
mend the hearts,
but never bring the love you lost.
When you vanished, I learned a
lesson:
I must gamble
even if my heart burns.

Ego

Some people never let their ego die. They sacrifice everything to satisfy their I, they feed its starving stomach with all the love and sincerity anyone would ever offer them. They are too persistent to accept what they see right as wrong or what they see dark as day. They accuse you for things you have never done and make you believe you were just a mistake in their life. To decorate their ego they would tear you layer by layer and make their selves pompous. We keep thinking they would change, they would miss us but then those people die with their ego lying on their chest like a medal. They never learn what they have lost, they never love what was meant to be loved and they never regret because their hearts were blind to see beyond their own selves.

Eulogy

All this love of days
and years,
I never asked to
love me back.
I never said
love me as do I.
Not a single word
of complaint.
Now when autumn
approaches and leaves
fall. No more blooms.
No more roses or
bright sky.
I wonder what if
I shall go too

unsung and unnoticed,
what if you never get time
to visit a cemetery?
Shall I be a little demanding?
And ask for something
before I die?
Perhaps, I will live
for a few more years
in your heart,
before I go deep down
in the ground
If only you can make an eulogy
for a Soul who loved you
as
the Sun
loves the horizon
without a sound.

Perfection

He was wild. He was untamed. He never talked smoothly. He wouldn't dress formally. He didn't know what to say at what time. He never bothered about taking photos on special occasions. He would just come, eat and never praise the food. He would never grip her hand when she held it. He never asked her to come back whenever she would try to reprimand him by leaving. He was cold. He was emotionless. He would hardly smile. He would sit calmly when she would cry.

He was furious as life hit him in every possible way. He was so unloved that it didn't matter to him if he broke her heart. He was her Hamlet, her mysterious Bermuda triangle. Yet he was so much loved by her, as if in this world anything perfect that existed for her, was he.

Demons

Demons don't go forth from the hearts where they were born; they leech there all day and set eyes on fire when night approaches. What do they hate most? Love! They never let you be loved, my dear. Never.

Adieu!

The Saint has gone, no more lullabies for me. The illusion has broken and the reflection says, every goodness which I tried to hold eventually had to go. That voice chanting in my ears for the last time. I cried my heart loudly with mute mourning. I burned the soul under the sun and reminded myself there is nothing I shall ever own. Adieu my love! Adieu!

Seeking Cure

In summer afternoon,
sitting among written fables,
I uncovered my hidden tale,
on a hope you would be my Hippocrates.
Today, I stand incurable
under the sun,
Wishing I was born
in the time of Jesus.

My Apple Tree

I sow an apple seed
and water it every day.
It was just my love for green,
I never wanted to own a tree.
When it started blooming,
I fell in love with every leaf.
Slowly its roots became stronger,
on its branches sat birds and bees.
I crossed my legs and sat under it,
I started worshiping it.
I spread my arms to catch the apples,
but it dropped stones
and let me bleed.

Irony

Yes losing love
is quite painful..
quite hurting.
It isn't sunshine.
It's a rainfall
and irony is
the only umbrella you find
is
your own self.

Infatuation

Who was she? Do you even remember her face, her eyes, her smile? Do you even remember you confessed you were madly and deeply in love with her? You have moved on and she is still riding the love on her wild untamed heart. That's what infatuation and love are all about.

If You

Should you take an initiative
and call and ask me to meet,
in a small coffee shop or at the corner of
Baskin and Robin's?
While you and I
wait for our order, perhaps we can
talk about the things we lost.
Or maybe we don't speak,
just let the silence
heal our wounds.
Just to be there would set all things right,
and the golden butterfly

would sit on our shoulders again.
If only you would ask. If only…

Drowned

To keep her soul
and heart safe
she drowned herself
in a muddy pond.
Her delicate being
soon became filthy
she started stinking.
Today, when she is untouchable,
unwanted and sinful,
you want her back.

Haunting Memories

Today, I opened up my diary,
blue as a sky.
The last page dated,
January 2nd 2015,
and the note said,
"Today, I discovered
He never loved, he just possessed.
He found the best so he left.
I can't walk home,
So I sit on a footpath
and cry my heart.
I called him an angel,
and he grew the wings.
He has flown and
I am going to die."

Seven months
flashed back.
Suicide failure,
pills and cigarettes.
sympathies and love,
in the name of caring
people taking advantage
of each other.
Crossing the road when
The signal was red,
honking cars and stumbling feet.
insomnia and kind friends.
Deleting your photos,
posting 'let it go' on every wall.
Today when he was just a memory,
he texted, confessing his love.
And with this blue journal,
I wonder,

will he ever erase
those seven months.

Wild Goose Chase

Who am I? I have lost all the answers to this question. It was he who defined me. His presence was my trait. It was his sound echoed in my laughter. To think of him would make my eyes glow, but now, I doubt my existence. I wonder if I am a mass of cells or an unseen soul. I wonder how it feels to smile? I question myself why he made me feel important, when I was accustomed to being unnoticed. I have stopped searching for him because I have realized it's a wild goose chase.

Deception

You still haunt me through different faces and you should be glad you aren't alone in this world. Who is so good at breaking hearts? There are people far more talented in playing 'love and break up' games than you. These are the people who claim to heal the broken hearts but smash it into tiny pieces. What pleasure do they get I could never figure it out? If someday you find your mind and heart in conflict then just come and let me know what pleasure deception gives?

Achievement

Seniors and juniors
all the boys loved her.
Not her, particularly,
but her delicate figure.
Tired of chasing her
they challenged Me,
as I was the hero of
many Eves.
And I succeeded by
mesmerizing her through
my words.
She lost all her soul
in my eyes.
And one day, I took her
in deserted area of the campus

to water her dry heart.
While I kissed her,
boys of my gang videotaped us.
After enough entertainment,
I whispered in her ears,
'Tomorrow there's a surprise
for you!'
She insisted to know,
But I let her go on a note,
'Few surprises are not meant
to wait for.'
Next day, our short porn movie
was on everyone's phone.
First in campus,
then in the city,
it was a famous show.
I never saw her after

our last wilderness date.
The surprise might have
surprised her at her place.
I never cared, I was
in the limelight.
Some called me
Kisser
a few named me asshole.
It was all an achievement,
until the day I heard the news,
that her cold body was found
swinging with the fan
in her bedroom.

Unsung

At the end we all die.
Some succumb to long illness,
while others to injuries
received in an accident.
But those who die in love,
remain unsung,
and unnoticed.
Despite how loud we sing
a love song,
at the end love is
unseen,
invisible
and
intangible.

Love and Hunger

Last night I told him
I can't take this anymore.
I can't play masquerade.
He said, he doesn't know
how to make me feel okay.

Okay? Darn! I want
to feel Loved NOT okay!

He started to touch me
from head to toe
without looking into my eyes.
You don't love me!
I concluded.

Teach me! Was what he asked.
My jaw dropped.
Teach love?
Love isn't taught,
it is felt in blood.
Do you feel me under your skin?
Do you feel hungry
at heart?
Don't misinterpret love
for lust.
Love doesn't come from
touch but from the most
vacant corners of the heart,
wherein resides
the hunger to know
we matter,
where eyes starve
to be seen

*to be read
with a serene
heart.*

I No More Cage Goodness

Were I fifteen-years old,
I would have chased you.
Pity, I have seen enough
dry wells.
Knocked by wolves
numberless time.
I can't close my eyes
to soothing lies
that sing to me.
I can't make one more
darling mistake.

I don't want to smile
on your flirtatious words.
I find it hard to breath
in this air of fake courtesy.
I'm aloof, cold and indifferent.
as you never happened to me,
as you don't exist.
because I no more
cage goodness.

The Girl Inside

I was a tom boy.
Not because I loved being a boy.
The limelight.
Yes it brought me lots of attention.
I would wander aimlessly
in summer afternoons
climbed the trees and
hit the boys.
I was Daddy's boy.
I turned eleven and mommy said,
No more jeans! No more shorts!
I cried all night and then decided
to dress traditionally
but, like a traditional boy.
The plain shirt wasn't enough

to hide my bosoms.
Wear a shawl and cover yourself
was daddy's order.
Time flew and slowly there were
no more trees or street games.
I tried to be a girl
who ought to stay home.
I lost my identity and Tom Boy
was dead,
but boys at my school
didn't know that.
To keep my embarrassment away,
I kept being rowdy at school.
I reached grade ten and boys
kept calling me 'Hey Bro!'
One day my buddy came home
to return the notebook
he borrowed in school.

Brother roared and father screamed.
Between the pages they found
a note, 'I love you please be mine!'
Daddy screamed and brother declared
Stay at home and no more school.
When darkness covered the limelight,
I met the Girl inside of me.

Horse Race

Everyone is in a race.
Not a horse race
or a race for money.
It's a new kind of race,
race of the 21st Century.
The damn race for *likes*.
Race of wearing a crown
on social sites.
Where relations are at stake.
Where emotions don't matter.
Where arguments are solved
not in private chats
but in public in form of
satirical *statuses*.
It's a race where love is

expressed on virtual *walls*.
Everyone feels the intensity
of love and happy care,
except one who is *tagged*
in romantic notes.
It's a strange race,
where it's never decided
who wins or loses.
A race that has interred
A physical world.
And I long for a *real* love.
in the world with only Horse Race!

The Lost Past

If I could bring the past back,
I would freeze those
sweet-strange moments
which grew on our sapling.
When I had you
with all your heart.
Nothing to hide,
nothing to worry.
When time wouldn't slip
like grains of sand.
When you never had to rush
like a train on platform.

If I knew love and you
were slipping from my hands
I would have frozen
You, Love and those seconds.

Compose New Song

I wonder
what do you tell her
about love.
The same things
which I heard once,
or have you composed
a new love song
with words and promises
unheard.

Pain

There comes a time
when we all stop growing.
We find peace in darkness,
silently turning us
possessive and demanding.
We envy, we cry,
we reach to the point
where loneliness appeals
more than a crowd.
Long never-ending catharsis
and cynical state,
frequent mood swings,
self-blaming and bullying
become a trait.

One day we get a push,
from a person who makes us believe
we are truly loved.
We matter too.
A person who cares day and night
who makes us feel special
by calling just to hear our voice.
And suddenly, overnight
love flies. Soon we fall in love
with our self, everything changes.
We realize that love was never possessed.
Darkness was never gone.
Eventually,
we meet this pain packed
inside a surprise package

it starts surrounding us with light.
And we are no more a cynic,
we don't cry anymore.
As we see things worse than
unreasonable depression.
At that very moment,
we leap into a mature adult.
In our twenties, we turn into
a thousand year old monument,
which has witnessed enough of
history,
which has felt and lost
this touch of love,
we become a person
who showers love
through pain absorbed.

You're Still Here

You forgot to take
one last thing,
You.

Tombstone

All these places where you exist,
my eyes on which
you have carved your name,
are calling you.
They call you
every time they see the roads
we crossed together,
a shore which we saw together,
the roof where we lay down
and counted the stars,
a garden where we
plucked the roses
that vase
on old wooden table,
they all make me ask for you.

Sooner or later, all these objects will vanish,
but my heart which is
a tombstone of your name,
will never vanish.

Library

Right here, right now
I'm missing you.
And to feel you
I walked to the library.
Remember? This place?
Where we met for first time.
Some books in front of you,
a newspaper in my hand.
From politics to civilization,
we switched our topics softly
to You and I.
We showed each other
our wounds
hidden behind our smiles.
Today, I got a new wound,

and I need you to see
so I sit here,
among the books of
finanace and marketing
wondering would you ever
come here. Perhaps,
just to read a newspaper
or for us?

Barriers of Sects

I never betrayed you.
I just loved you
the way I should have.
I loved you in ways,
I was allowed to.
Betrayal wasn't in my blood.
Those were high walls of
this prison.
You couldn't see them,
because I never showed you the
custom in which I breathe.
I chose to worship Love
like the sun, which peeps in my
yard, but never dared to

stay in my arms.
I sang to you like a sparrow,
which perched on my window,
but too afraid to step inside, I had to leave you,
since the walls of our love
were made of bricks
called *sects*.

I Cut the Roots of Love

I gave up on us.
I eschewed love.
A love which I craved for.
It wasn't easy.
It can never be easy
to shun what you love.
But at the end
It is better to
cut the sapling
which is supposed to
grow and fall on the
roof of your house.

Reversal

It is just a matter of time
when we all can heal
as if we have never been broken,
as if we have never
been in love,
as if freedom was
all that we had,
as if tears have never
been our companion,
but it's just
a question of timing.

Section Two
Pronoun

Change

I would always complain
of people changing,
their love vanishing overnight.
I sometimes had the courage
to tell them it hurts
to see them change.
I was told softly, rudely and
sometimes angrily
that they haven't changed.
It is their situation
which has changed.
The pain would poison
my whole being
wondering why the situation

never changed me or
the expression of my love.
Slowly I got used to their
frequent absence
the day came when
they disappeared
completely
but it never hurt.
I accepted this change with
a plethora of strength
that finally
I changed myself.
I realized this when I saw them
again.
That time,
my heart didn't beat fast,
tears never swam in my eyes.

Today, nothing moves me
if I see their photos
or hear their name
whispered on someone else's lips.

Today I smile and don't question
why people change
because,
we all do.
We have to.
That is how we are
designed to.
Some take initiative to change first
while other are compelled
to change as
standing water always stinks.

Two Words

Today, after giving up,
I wrote two words.
The words which are
rainless clouds.
The words which are
the summary of my love.
And it seems as if
I have forgotten
how to read, write
and speak.
And these two words
will be my only expression.
My only request,
like the shattered, broken
story of my love.

These words are
the moist of my eyes.
my lost smile,
the weariness of my face.
They are,
my profit, my loss,
my prize, my defeat
and today, after losing the battle
and falling on my knees
among the corpse of lovers,
I have waved a flag with
two words,
Come Back!

Promise

I might not be able to take
all your sorrows but
I promise at the end of
each day
your comfort zone
will always be
my lap.
I'd quietly listen to
all the heartaches and
before you would step
into the land of dreams,
I'd whisper:
"I shall always love you."

Knock

In the middle of the night
while climbing down
the stairs of my house,
I ponder
how shall I accept
how the sun-rays are
knocking on the door of
my pitch-black house.

Worries

While I'm sipping my morning coffee,
I hear a bunch of youngsters sitting in a cafe and
arguing on some rules of phonetics. Each one coming up
with a valid point and each one trying to prove another wrong.
Laptops opened in front of them, and one holding Advance Learner's Dictionary.
One says it's AN Historian,
and others say it's A Historian.
Explanations given in context of

vowels and consonants.
As rising steam from my coffee
fogs my glasses, I wonder
how blessed our lives would be
if the only things
which could worry us were
A or AN.

Letter

Dear Myself,

I apologize from the core of my heart for hurting you every day. You've suffered in harsh days and during miserable nights. I'm sorry for giving you to the people who never deserved you. People who never treated you the way you meant to be.

Today, I want to love you, I want to give you all that love which you've missed all life because you're important, you matter, you're special. You're strong, beautiful, kind and patient. Now you won't suffer silently, as I shall love you till eternity.

Yours, I

Sea

I have a sea,
a sea of questions
which smile, hate and cry.
A sea which glows
and flows to sweep off
my pain and sorrows.
A sea which can take
my breath away.
A sea which gives me
reason to live. A sea
which I see in his eyes.
There I live,
there I shall die.

Life's Art

I imagined love
existing by the seashore.
I would think
it is holding hands all night
or it might be looking
into each other's eyes,
or humming the love song and
asking to sing.
I would think love is
walking in green fields
and I was going
to see the stars all night,
after a few kisses
and some cuddles,
love opened a new door of magic.

Magic in the name of reality,
which washed all the fancy
dreams.
And I learned more
than making love.
It's making home,
rather than seeing stars
it's mopping floors.

Love isn't ease
but a toil and hard work.
It's not romantic
but conversations
on bills and notes.
All these years
love never faded;
even when there were
no stars and no seashore.
Love stays and grows

if the world is seen
with open eyes
and a forgiving heart
while accepting life's imperfect art.

Huma Adnan

Games

Little I was,
smaller were the
games.
More I grew,
so did they.

Child

It was hard to let my bird fly,
hiding tears and composing;
to let it go with joy and serenity.
I smiled till it hurt me,
on the hope that it will be safe
and return to the place
where it belongs,
so I let my heart and soul
be its companion
rather than words
of farewell or gloominess.
And I wait
till the day it comes back,
so I shall sing the lullabies,
once more and

all over
till eternity.

Reader's Soul

I wonder
if my soul has travelled
from the garden
where Hardy walked,
or from the desk
where Austen penned
the love story of
Elizabeth and Darcy,
or is it from the hearth
where Brontë imagined
Cathy and Heathcliff.
I am not from this age.
I imagine love,
In ballrooms.
among tulips

on piano's notes.

I imagine love
in secrets,
in fear
with modesty
yet bold.

Free Bird

There are people who are so decent and classy. I'm not like them. I can only be sophisticated in meetings and interviews. I can't use knives and forks on the table every day. Sometimes I walk on the road barefoot. I don't care about jewellery and clothes. I never mind sitting on dirt. I can wear the same pair of jeans for days. I am a free bird but people like me find it hard to fit in society. The world needs class while I need nature. All these cities were once a wilderness, so my soul is from nature not from skyscraper. While many wish for a lavish life, all I desire is a cottage among the fields, a meal enough for two, and love to keep us warm and safe. I can't change myself because this is a post-modern age. I've had enough of technology and class. If you need a perfect person, I'm sorry I disregard rules. Rules aren't made for me.

Treader

This life does not stop,
if someone comes or leaves.
Apparently loneliness whispers,
but not for long.
This life is like a pathway,
people walk and go.
Would it be wise to expect
every treader to stay?
You are an important
part of my life.
But my life is like a
poppy flower,
surrounded by dreariness.
And I wonder
where are you?

but I have learnt
the art of
spending the nights alone.
Yet there are few tears
which often call your name
like a pampered baby.
But one day,
they will learn
they must stop rolling down
as life doesn't stop
nor the treader.

Peace

I hope that silence will
find a meaning and
would let the fears fly.
All that has been
eaten by demons
will start healing
and one day,
we all shall be
in peace.

Sonnets for Me

Today, I don't want to
write about you,
love or
memories
we made.
But the beauty existing
in my soul.
which was left unsung
by you and
by me.
Today, I shall praise it
and admire the fact
how blissful life was
and is.
No matter how painfully

you carved your name
on my heart.
I have freed my soul
and I shall move on
with a sonnet
written solely for me.

Erudite

Today I can parry,
as once I had accumulated
into darkness.
The vulpine words,
have apprehended me for long.
It's a blessing that,
feelings cannot be synthesized
or else you would have,
interred my heart. I perceive,
I haven't been talented.
Today with my hoarse voice,
I claim life with facility.
In multifaceted phases
I was left unsung.
No one to confer,

but today I am released,
and I'm able to speculate
that in life,
you sometimes need to gamble,
you need to purloin the smiles;
and sanction your soul from body.
You need to enunciate all your
Emotions and deaden them;
coddle the love inside your heart
and proscribe it from withering.
You must burgeon your soul and
leave it to disport; either
it vanquishes or remains esoteric
for the world
Surely it will
remain antithetical,
and yet at the end

you will be
Erudite.

Only Me

I am here among the stars under
the sky.
The cold breeze heals my wounds.
It seems
there was no past with any pain,
no future to worry for.
All is present
in the present with
me and only me.

Heaven

There's a world
quite vivid and clear.
And there's a world
I wish to see,
hiding the souls
which once were tangible.
The world where
life and death
have no meaning.

Probably

Mom,
I have no control over
time and heart.
In one evening of July
I couldn't stop time,
and after fifteen years,
I can't run my heart.
They both are stubborn
from ages.
One loves to run
and other likes to stop
like a static sun
and the moving earth,
one worships fire
and the other bows to dust.

Together they hurt me a lot.

and tonight,
you come in my dream
and ask not to cry.
How is it possible
heart stops beating and
the needles of a clock
are broken?
I wonder,
why I can't forget that evening
when before leaving you said,
Don't annoy daddy!
Don't fight with bro!
I kept waiting
probably you would say,
Take care of yourself!
probability grew deeper

in my heart and I wished
to kiss your forehead,
but I froze and time ran.
I left you alone and
walked home.
At ten, the phone rang
and my heart boded
Probably, you are gone!
I hid behind the door,
peeped inside the hall,
Saw my brother crying.
He was saying something,
probably telling daddy
to bring you home.
And then you came,
with cold hands
and a lifeless body,

which I kissed
from head to toe,
probably for the last time.

That moment I shed
no tears, but Mom
I am drained today
and something is missing.
Probably,
a heart has no needles
and time has no ropes,
but there is probability
in my heart
that you are still here
for the flower
I plucked from your grave,
leave me with your fragrance
even today.

Karma

I know I would
keep moving, breathing
and living.
I have accepted
that you are gone.
Your departure has
cleared the mist of
fake promises and love.
You have been replaced
by sunshine
but do you know,
you will always carry
the fog of lies and betrayal
in your heart?
It's just a matter of time

when they will become
visible.

Burning Hearts

How red coal heats the cold
shivering body.
It soothes and comforts us
while burning
on untouchable fire.
Just like the pain,
the gain in love.
Like the hearts
burned in vain.

Question

What went wrong?
A question I ask myself
several times.
You loved me
as I always wanted to be loved.
And it was the most perfect one.
A love I longed for.
A love no one has ever owned.
I started worshipping you
and made you
my church,
my temple,
my mosque.
And there all went wrong.
God took away all the love

from your heart and
I was forgotten and lost
as if we had never met.
As if you never loved.

Three Tricky Words

I want to keep you in my life till eternity, so I will hide my love deep down in my heart, I will never let you know how much I miss you when you are not around. I will paint you with my wildest imagination and hang on the top of my heart. You will reflect through my eyes, smile and poetry. But I shall never say those three tricky words, as I fear to lose you. As you are my hope. As you are mine!

Just Love

Hide yourself beneath my heart,
as twosome hid under the moon
with their souls tied in one,
nothing to parry but just love.

Come

Come,
touch my soul.
Find me, discover me.
whisper,
talk,
speak to me.
Water the thorns
cool the sun,
Come,
bring me peace.

Ashes

The hoar around your heart
doesn't let you see
a person shattering day by day
in your love.
It doesn't let you feel
the warmth of love
which could keep you safe
for eternity.
Call my heart arson
as this state of being unnoticed
is slowly setting my soul on fire.
Who will collect the ashes
and will you scatter them
at Ganges?

Letter to My Girl

Dear Girl,

Be a lady! You have tried enough, haven't you? I know the ego kills relationships and rots the love, but what if a sailor doesn't need your help to save their drowning ship? How many times did you knock on the door? Twice, thrice more than that? Isn't that enough? Bowing shouldn't be your trait but forgiving should be. There will be people telling you that 'Move On' is a strong word and do you really mean to use it? Tell them YES you

mean it! For in the end, either you break into two or into tiny shards,
you will be the only one to mend yourself. Be strong and accept what's gone. If they love you then no storm would stop them reaching you, they don't need pigeons to bring a letter. They are as equipped with technology as you are. You have used this little electronic more than enough for reconciliation, if they truly love you, a small text would never be bigger than their ego. You just have to be strong because you are always loved!

Love,
A Lady who has been a girl once.

You have..

Loneliness isn't corroding if one is never too alone and no one is too lonely. You have You!

Don't Rot Your Soul

Have you ever seen standing water?
It starts stinking after a few days.
It produces moss not blooms.
So do bitter memories.
The longer you stick to them,
the more you rot your soul.

Love over Lust

I would have given you my soul,
my entire being and each breath
if you had loved my scars
more than the transitory skin.

Immortal

You have expressed love
with the silence,
which made my heartbeat
sonorous.
And I have loved you,
with mellifluous poetry
which has made us immortal.
We shall not fear death anymore.

Survivor

If you choose to detach yourself from me, I would never come and beg you to stay. If you tend to forget all the promises ever made then believe me, I will never remind you. I will slowly move back without a single word of complaint. I would go back where I had come from and it won't take me long to be in the company of nature in desolation. I grew up in a valley surrounded by spectacular mountains, trees and waterfalls. They never responded when I sang my heart to them. You see, I would never mind the echo of my own footsteps. I will listen to my own heartbeat with a smile which you have tried to take away in the name of cure. You are free to replace, ignore or leave me, for I am survivor and I have seen worst! I don't shed tears anymore!

Differences and Our Love

It was only yesterday when
love knocked on our heart
with delicacy.
It kissed our soul
and opened the doors of paradise
led us to the journey to infinity.
We loved from distance and today,
We are the pillars of one house.
Despite our differences we have,
a tendency to love, care and live
while holding each other in our
hearts.

Light Your World

Sometimes you have to leave your comfort zone and walk on unknown paths to explore why your tiny mini little heart is always ready to break you into little pieces by exploding itself and tearing the soul apart. You probably won't find the answers on stones and graffiti on the walls but you will learn that those you lost aren't far from you, they're moving in your very own shadow.

You don't need to text and wait in the middle of the night to every person in your phone list with two painful words 'need you', rather by walking on unfamiliar ways you need to tell yourself that you need yourself the most! Stop waiting for someone to open the door and take you out into the sunshine. You aren't a baby anymore. Get up and light up the darkness believing that love resides within you.

Butterfly

I'm certain,
we both are no more the same.
No more half
not even a quarter.
I do love you,
but don't miss you.
I don't cry anymore,
I don't even notice if you ignore.
I see your photos no more,
I have placed your present
at the back of a shelf.
And do you know?
My heart doesn't jump
even if it sees those souvenirs.
You never needed love,

because the need of love,
makes us lovers not ignorant.
And with your aloofness
you made me cold,
and stronger than before.
Perhaps, I have learnt,
to be a butterfly than a cocoon.

Words of Love

I won't repeat,
a single word of love.
As love was never
meant to be understood
by you, My Love.

I Love You Mercilessly

I imagine vain love.
Attempts to be with you
in unlikely situations.
I imagine crawling into your
dreams
or sitting by you when you're
asleep.
Oh yes, I imagine peculiar things.
But merciless too.
I imagine you falling sick,
and I, only I, being the one
to take care of you.
To protect you to an extent
that when you open your eyes
you fall in love with me

not just for that moment

but for eternity.
Yes I do curse myself
for putting you in pain
in these unrealistic thoughts.
But does the heart listen?
Does it ever lull to sleep?
Honey, it tosses and turns
and rests only in a grave.
As I write these journals on a hope
that one day you will read
and know how much you really
mean.

Magician!

You love me as a
giant rock on a shore,
touched by waves
every day.
Strong and weak tides,
never let it move.
You reside in my heart
so firmly.
You breath in me,
sleep in me.
You are a magician
who knows how to
tear me apart and
make me whole.
Oh Love! use your

magic and dissolve me
within you!
So I may no more be
on seashore,
but a seashell
living in you.

You are Sunshine!

You feel lonely sometimes,
don't you?
And you feel there's
no one in this world who exists
for you only? Or sometimes,
you think loneliness is all you have.
Your parents gave up on you or
you never had a chance to know
who your parents were.
You couldn't hug your daddy
as your friends did.
You never felt the warmth
of a mother's love in what they call
a home

Then you fell in love and dreamt of love,

a home, beautiful children, busy city life
and to move somewhere among mountains and trees after retirement.
You dreamt but it never became reality.
You didn't commit suicide
not because you didn't give up,
since suicide was too painful
and you decided to live.
Did you try to break the walls
of loneliness and climb out to see a bright new day?
Why did you never stand in front

of a mirror and tap the shoulder
of that strong person who trans-
formed so bravely?

Doesn't that person deserve f
a few words
of praise?
A soul so hard that even the sky
doubts
the strength of typhoons.
You felt lonely all this time,
while there lived a thunder in you,
who made it so far
and who is a sunshine today.

Reunion

It was my birthday,
surrounded by friends.
Presents, music, laughter,
perfection for the rest
but my heart sighed.
My eyes craved for that
particular person.
He arrived and a gust of wind
touched my face.
We greeted each other
like strangers.
He sat next to me
and we exchanged
few formal words.
Slowly everyone left.

The party ended.
He stayed.
He had so much to say,
I had so much to ask.
He didn't. I couldn't.
We met, we parted
without a smile.

I was told by my family
and friends to move on.
I tried, I failed.
Moving on is tiring.
It brings memories closer
than before. More than
moving on, it was holding tight.
One day, while dusting
a bookshelf.
I opened a book, a present

from him and found
his photo.
Putting my thought away,
I captured the photo from my phone
and sent him with a text,
"Saw you. After long time."
A minute later he replied,
"Yes I remember this,
you took that from my wallet."

The chaos ended.
Peace returned.
As things never went wrong.
As I never let my heart
be dissected mercilessly by
a few painful memories.

Jinx

I don't remember if ever in life
I experienced a moment
as magical as being in love
with you.

I can't recall if I ever had
been in trance as
magnetic as your love.

You were a magician
or love was a jinx.
Maybe your eyes cast a spell.

And here I am
in utter madness.
Craving for more.

Starving to hear
your voice which could
soothe the rhythm of my soul.

And in this starvation
I've forgotten
how merciless love is.
How cruel you can be.

Trust Your Instincts

Eyes have so much to say
and a heart has so much to cry for.
Let's meet by the seashore
and for some time
we follow our instincts.
And fall in love
while I cry,
while you shiver.
I soothe you
and you comfort me.
Let our darkest corners
be our eternal light.

Enemies

I don't mind carrying you
in my heart all my life.
I know feelings don't jingle,
they can't make noise
to wake up the drowsy,
drunken heart.
They can only love silently
and if fate is on my side
I will probably win you.
I might carve my name
on your heart.
But fate and I are
enemies since my childhood.

Since ages.
Before I loved you.
Before you loved her.

One Day

Love dances and hearts cry.
What if a soul shatters
and night flies?
No day to remorse.
No night to shed tears.
Love in the arms of a heart
dances and call the lovers
to fill in love
again and again.
Silently you will be mine.
But it all can happen
if the earth stops moving
and the angels sleep.

On the Peak

I relive the love
when you warm me
with your presence.
When together we stand
on the peak of the mountains
and stare at the city
below us.

His Voice

Sometimes I call him without a reason. I don't even have words to say. I just want to hear his voice and let it enter in my brain, flow through my nerves and reach the heart. On other side of the phone I just stand and smile and never want to break that spell.

My Poetry

He asked, "Have you ever written anything for him?"
"He is in each and every word of my poem and prose." I replied.

Still Loved

There was nothing in him which I didn't love. His heart, soul, eyes, hands and words. Yes, the very words which broke my heart. But each shard still loves him. Every time when my heart beats, the shards bleed my heart, but the flow of love is stronger than the pain received.

Reader

He reads me as I am a book written solely for him. He turns each page delicately in a fear I might not tear.

Healer

I want to heal you
for once and all,
he whispered.
'We can't leave the ones
who heal our hearts.
At least I can't, but when your
priorities change, they
leave behind the darkest scars.'

He smiled and shook his head,
The choices which change,
are not to be called priority.
If you are ever replaced,
then you never were one.

Prayer

Lord!
Dissolve me
And dissolve him
And dissolve our souls
Today, tomorrow, for an eternity.

A Tribute to a Fierce Lover

Yes I write for him.
I write for *he* or *his*.
He exists in my each word.
In my poetry and prose.
You see, the world is too blind
to see the goodness in him.
His aggressive face has
a story to tell.
His swollen eyes have
travelled a journey for miles.
He still has a heart to love
but a tongue which can't express.
What he gives on way of love
goes unnoticed.
The dark circle around his eyes

is considered part of his face.
He is ought to be a gentleman,
but he is a warrior,
facing discrimination everyday
for having strong bones.
His efforts, his struggle
and his love have been suppressed
in the name of reality.
I write for him,
he chose to love,
but remained unsung.
I put him in my verses
as I chose to love him
but can't make the world
fall in love with him.
I shall give the words
to his unsaid love.
May it be a tribute.

Pleasure

He loves what pleases his heart.
A pet, a book,
a phone or
a person.
But he loves them,
as long as they
please him.
and the painful thing is
pleasure doesn't last
forever.

Take Me Away

I texted him
"Take me away"
He was too busy to reply.
Today, when we met
after many days.
I leaned on his shoulder,
held his hand,
and put them on my eyes,
with a bright smile
like he was the sun
and I was the moon,
he glanced at me
and lightened up my face.
He whispered softly,
'Why do you always touch

my hands on your eyes.'
I dissolve my soul
in your skin,
so when you go,
you don't leave me behind.

Normal Life

He loves me
through words
through
silence.
I love him,
with passion,
with fire.
Yet he prefers
to see me
going mad
in his love
while he lives
a normal life
with
her.

Moth

He heals me
like a magician.
I burn in his love
like a moth.

Daddy's Boy

His daddy hit his mom
when he was four.
The events never ended,
and he never learnt
how to love.

We met and
I found him fierce.
I wanted to be the Beauty
to heal the Beast.

Years passed by,
he loved me like a
lost child
seeking home.

Huma Adnan

Today, he saw me
talking to the guy from the
neighbourhood,
inviting us to his sister's birthday.

I returned home,
and he threw the vase.
A moment later,
I was on the floor.

Blood running
down my legs,
as I lost our child,
I shivered and cried.

The prince turned back
 into the beast.
Since he was the cactus,
 his daddy grew.

Lover of Glow

He was as lonely as a cave man.
Needing my company,
because I would laugh.
I was loquacious and
a jolly soul.
I made him happy like
a three year old.
He longed for someone
with a free soul
to fill the cracks of his dark life.
Slowly I lost the glitter
of my wings.
as I was drenched in love,
from head to toe.
My reasons to smile were

confined to one.
His presence was the only source
of my laughter.
Those little things
friends, silly jokes, or ice cream
cones,
didn't appeal to me anymore.
He couldn't bear
my over-protective-love and
I-miss-you notes.
he found a fairy with
the sparkling glow
and left me in shades of
day and night snow.

Promise

He asked her to
Promise something,
She was scared but she nodded.
Never let that curve on your face die.
That night she didn't sleep.
She smiled all night.

Love Him

He is fierce
for what he went through.
He is unexplainable
and drenched in pain
as he is hiding all the scars.
All pain is painted with
a charade of happiness.
If you really love him,
then stay.
He will love you
more than angels,
more than
you've ever been
loved!

Unloved

He triumphs!
As there are few
who survive in love.
You had no intention
to save him.
He discovered the magic
among the haters.
Today, he is healed
like he was never injured
and you never
wounded him.

After Years

He wasn't so magical,
but I was in love
and made him the only man
in the universe.
I loved him more than
I understood love.
He, on the other hand,
couldn't contemplate
the feelings I hid.

I was a girl,
sleeping with his used shirt,
stealing his toothbrush and comb.
A girl drinking
the leftover water from his glass.

Asking him to eat,
half of her chocolate first.
For me, love was to merge the souls.
While for him,
I was a stubborn child,
who never grows up.
He tried to explain Love
through logics and theories.
Finally, nothing worked
and we quietly broke.

Today, he isn't magical for me.
But sometimes he texts,
Your Love was magical.

Unaware

He dreams to touch the sunset,
to freeze the hue of dawn
in her eyes.

What he sees is today's reality.
Unaware that future has
its own colours.

Tomorrow he would own
a new planet with
a new sun.

Glitter and Light

One of his most circumspect action is
to distant himself
from her,
but the results took away
the glitter of her eyes
and
the light of his life.

Section Three
Love and Something

Love Flows

We fall in love
with each other's perfection
and to keep the love alive,
we start loving flaws.
Thus, making love
eternal.

Expiry date

We are often promised that we won't be hurt and left alone. We shall be loved and cared. They call us life, soul or heart. When they utter these words they truly mean it, but we need to remember words don't come with an expiry date.

Cherish Each Moment

Each moment is an art.
A hot shower
on a cold day,
a steaming cup of coffee,
a gust of air
under sunlight,
the aroma of freshly baked cake,
running stream,
evaporated mirror,
a good fragrance,
crispy bed sheets,
floating clouds,
smell of rain,
moonlight.
So much of art

by an Unseen Artist
to make us cherish
each second
and to let go
what's gone
or what was never yours.

Listen

Be silent and listen to the welkin falls,
here you are lost
and grounds have flown.
Listen to the thunders
which reside in every soul.
Watch the one who is dying of hunger and thirst.
Carve your name on the zenith,
on the nadir are graves of lost gone.
Aim is right there in a heart which sighs,
Break the cage and spread the wings in sky.

Sing the melody with trembling lips,
that aches for that unforgettable kiss.
There on the sky He sits and watches,
fill the void and hold the Ubiquitous Lord!

Unfathomable Relation

It's an unfathomable relation,
as between light and shadow.
The craving of desert for a cloud,
like a lost traveller's love for moon.
A fisherman standing with his boat
by the shore.
A sparrow bird fallen from its nest,
somehow that is
what is my essence,
it's an unfathomable relation.

Memories

Our most faded memories reside deep down inside us; it just takes a fraction of a second to make our souls travel back to the long gone days either through an old photo, a familiar place or smell of a new notebook.

The Way We Love

One day
we all will be loved
the way we love.

Right Love

What a joy
to discover
the right path,
right people
and
right love.

Love Will Do

Evince your love,
like a bard,
dancing on each verse,
pervasive in every word.
Sing to me your love,
as you are a nightingale
and I am your Keats.
Tread with me as
this world is vernal,
with no winter or snow
but daisies and glow.
Salvage the future
and grow the tree of love.
Just hold my hand
and love will do its best.

Bond

Love is a free bird, it's a feeling despite being near or far. It's an emotion which doesn't take us away from others but makes us love each and everything in this world. Often in love people turn aloof forgetting that love means giving in all directions and not only to one particular person. If we are not capable of loving everyone then we are not under love but possession. Love is not being selfish it's being kind and humble.

Wait

Let me stand here and wait
for pleasing spring and state,
when birds fly around my head,
bring me roses and bade adieu.

Autumn passes, summer burns.
Night lure as days must run,
with taciturn moon and mystic sun.
But I shall wait until thee come!

The Artist

Falling in love is just as you are
a new paint brush and God dips
you in different colours, passionately paints an abstract, beautiful and
unexplainable art
in a single stroke.
Thus leaving you encrusted
with dry paint
and unusable
for days to come.

Loving One's Self

Loving one's self is the hardest thing. It takes a lot. It is to be alone without expecting a call or text message. It's keeping your phone like a normal electronic rather checking it time and again. It's baking a chocolate brownie solely for yourself. It's standing in a theatre queue to buy a single ticket for a show being surrounded by love birds. It's sitting in a busy restaurant and eating without feeling alone. Learning to love one's company might not be easy but worth it. Explore yourself, love those parts of your body which can't be reached by any other human. Smile and tap your shoulder once you spend a day without any expectations. A human body is capable of doing a lot more than one's imagination can grasp. It is far stronger than the roots of a century's old juniper tree. It is more magical than the lights showered by angels. It is far flexible than any molding liquid. All it needs is a test, a time and exploration.

Embracing Morning

We all have stormy nights.
When we crouch down
and cuddle our pillow.
We cry till thunder stops.
But we all are loins
with every rising morning.
Like we never cry.
As life treats us
with royal acclaim.

Hope and Love

Hope is hale and hearty
yet it chooses
to love hopelessly
now and then.

Bomb Blast

I was born in a valley,
a symbol of norms and rules.
Surrounded by spectacular mountains
touched by cold breezes every day.
Mellifluous water of the fountains.
Peace, serenity and nature was
the canvas of God and our home.
I miss the apricot gardens,
apples and cherries,
listening to fables about fairies.
Eating hot soup in
snowy winter evenings,
climbing trees in the yard
but freedom lasted
till I reach twenty-six.
For those eyes I never was a human.

I was a girl, a woman, a lady.
A boy following me back home
from school and a brother doubting
my chastity. Desperate men
touching me in market places
even if I covered myself in blue
with a gown from head to toe.
Joining university was another struggle,
convincing brothers, requesting dad.
Finally I completed my bachelors,
but my starving soul asked for more.
I became rebellious and
stepped into the university for a Master's,
while pursuing my dreams,
I forgot I was followed by devils…
One day, after my final exam
I bid good-bye to my friends

*with laughter and chuckles
and walked towards the iron gate.
God wasn't smiling on that day
as usual I wasn't late.
Within a second my world exploded,
with a sound of bang I was torn into pieces.
Someone had planted a bomb in the bus
of the Women's World
and set the books
on fire along with us.
For the sake of religion or a war
I could never know, but death brought
more disappointment as the world
never noticed the bloodshed in June.*

Kodak

Such a strange feeling
reading faces.
Sit in a café and observe
the eyes searching for love.
Look at their lips.
Some with a curve
and others with a flat line.
What are they thinking
remains unheard.
But just observing them
gives a sense of
how fast the world moves.

Years ago, people would
sit and talk.

Today, they don't want to
miss a situation
to take photos and make them
part of their public gallery.
During seminars
or if it's a regular ice cream.
A wedding or watching
a boring movie. No one
misses a chance of
clicking photos.
I look back and wonder
is it a blessing or a curse
to be born in the eighties,
and missing so many records
of a life
as Kodak film was
far out of reach on my budget.

My Land

It's a land of
poets, artists and kings,
who eloquently left behind
their tradition, thoughts
and verses
on the walls
of palaces, castles and mosques.
It's a land of lovers
and the home of Iqbal.
It's a meadow where lovers meet
secretly and in silence.
A place where mothers give birth
to stars and moons.
Where dawn caresses a ground
with splendid four seasons.

Huma Adnan

A place where mountains
meet rivers and the sky touches
K2 and kisses the fountains.
Yet it's so unknown
to the world who call it
a war zone.

War

War wasn't when
they bombed us
and turned our houses
into rubble.

It wasn't when
we left the home
and crossed the border
to the land unknown.

The war wasn't
when I became
a widow at the age of
twenty-four.

Huma Adnan

It was when I sold myself
for a hundred bucks
to feed my
three starving angels.

Park

Red.
Blue.
Skirts.
Trousers.
Green grass.
Soothing Breeze.
People jogging.
Children running.
Falling leaves.
Wooden benches.
Sitting under the trees.
What life exists round me.
I wish,
the whole world
was a Park.

My Soul

It's unfathomable
like the sun and shadow's
companionship
in June.
A desert's desire
for a cloud
in summer noon.
A lost traveler's need
in the dark forest
for a moon.
A sailor standing
by the shore
with his broken boat.

A fallen bird hatching
from the nest
seeking home.

Such is my soul.

You can find more of author's work on:
www.humadnan.com
Instagram: @athousandyearsoflearning
Facebook: A Thousand Years of Learning

A Note for My Crafters

This is something like an acknowledgment with plenty of names, but I can't help it, as I am crafted by many hands throughout my life. Firstly, thank you to all, some who parted by death, others by fate and a few by consciousness. Behind each of us there are many hands who raise us and some who groom us. There are people who change us through love and others by pain. They both deserve thanks, since love and pain together make a poet. Thank you Mom and Dad, who are in heaven for bringing me into this world. Haroon, for raising me like a mom and dad. Miss Rohma, for showing me I can love, Sir

Saji, for telling me that I can write. My editor Christina, thank you for your encouragement and support. All my teachers, Ms. Naveeda, Saba Zaidi, Saba Amin, Shaista, Fouzia Rahman, Madheea Fazal, Dr. Akhtar Aziz and all those who built me at each step of my life, thank you for your constant encouragement! Kinza, for being you! Hasnat, the best cousin! Sara Warraich, for your continuous support. Dan, for helping me when I couldn't find solutions. Ayuuz, my baby-brother, for giving few irreplaceable-magical moments. All my friends, students and readers who always motivate me! My Instagram and Facebook followers thank you for your support. Sarah Doughty, Sarah Price for appreciating my work when I began to write. Thank you Abrar, Christina, Chris, Alfa, Jay and Jimmy for always showing me the way to light and thank you my entire poets' family. I love you all! And Dear God, Thank you for creating this world!

www.ingramcontent.com/pod-product-compliance
Lightning Source LLC
Chambersburg PA
CBHW050533300426
44113CB00012B/2083